# PROFESSIONAL ORCHESTRATION

## ORCHESTRAL SKETCHBOOK

8.3 X 11.7, 16-STAVE PLUS PERCUSSION, PRE-RULED, 4 BARS PER PAGE

ALEXANDER PUBLISHING

Training That Gets Results

ALEXANDER PUBLISHING
Petersburg, Virginia

**visit us at www.professionalorchestration.com**

ISBN 978-0-939067-68-8


Manufactured in the United States of America
Alexander Publishing, P.O. Box 1720 Petersburg, VA 23805

# PROJECT NOTES

Piccolo /
Flute

Oboe /
English Horn

Clarinet

Bassoon /
Bass Clarinet

French
Horns

Trumpets

Trombones /
Tuba

Timpani

Percussion

Violin I

Violin II

Violas

Cellos

Basses

Piccolo /
Flute

Oboe /
English Horn

Clarinet

Bassoon /
Bass Clarinet

French
Horns

Trumpets

Trombones /
Tuba

Timpani

Percussion

Violin I

Violin II

Violas

Cellos

Basses

Piccolo /
Flute

Oboe /
English Horn

Clarinet

Bassoon /
Bass Clarinet

French
Horns

Trumpets

Trombones /
Tuba

Timpani

Percussion

Violin I

Violin II

Violas

Cellos

Basses

Piccolo /
Flute

Oboe /
English Horn

Clarinet

Bassoon /
Bass Clarinet

French
Horns

Trumpets

Trombones /
Tuba

Timpani

Percussion

Violin I

Violin II

Violas

Cellos

Basses

Piccolo /
Flute

Oboe /
English Horn

Clarinet

Bassoon /
Bass Clarinet

French
Horns

Trumpets

Trombones /
Tuba

Timpani

Percussion

Violin I

Violin II

Violas

Cellos

Basses

Piccolo /
Flute

Oboe /
English Horn

Clarinet

Bassoon /
Bass Clarinet

French
Horns

Trumpets

Trombones /
Tuba

Timpani

Percussion

Violin I

Violin II

Violas

Cellos

Basses

Piccolo /
Flute

Oboe /
English Horn

Clarinet

Bassoon /
Bass Clarinet

French
Horns

Trumpets

Trombones /
Tuba

Timpani

Percussion

Violin I

Violin II

Violas

Cellos

Basses

Piccolo /
Flute

Oboe /
English Horn

Clarinet

Bassoon /
Bass Clarinet

French
Horns

Trumpets

Trombones /
Tuba

Timpani

Percussion

Violin I

Violin II

Violas

Cellos

Basses

Piccolo /
Flute

Oboe /
English Horn

Clarinet

Bassoon /
Bass Clarinet

French
Horns

Trumpets

Trombones /
Tuba

Timpani

Percussion

Violin I

Violin II

Violas

Cellos

Basses

Piccolo /
Flute

Oboe /
English Horn

Clarinet

Bassoon /
Bass Clarinet

French
Horns

Trumpets

Trombones /
Tuba

Timpani

Percussion

Violin I

Violin II

Violas

Cellos

Basses

Piccolo /
Flute

Oboe /
English Horn

Clarinet

Bassoon /
Bass Clarinet

French
Horns

Trumpets

Trombones /
Tuba

Timpani

Percussion

Violin I

Violin II

Violas

Cellos

Basses

Piccolo /
Flute

Oboe /
English Horn

Clarinet

Bassoon /
Bass Clarinet

French
Horns

Trumpets

Trombones /
Tuba

Timpani

Percussion

Violin I

Violin II

Violas

Cellos

Basses

Piccolo /
Flute

Oboe /
English Horn

Clarinet

Bassoon /
Bass Clarinet

French
Horns

Trumpets

Trombones /
Tuba

Timpani

Percussion

Violin I

Violin II

Violas

Cellos

Basses

Piccolo /
Flute

Oboe /
English Horn

Clarinet

Bassoon /
Bass Clarinet

French
Horns

Trumpets

Trombones /
Tuba

Timpani

Percussion

Violin I

Violin II

Violas

Cellos

Basses

Piccolo /
Flute

Oboe /
English Horn

Clarinet

Bassoon /
Bass Clarinet

French
Horns

Trumpets

Trombones /
Tuba

Timpani

Percussion

Violin I

Violin II

Violas

Cellos

Basses

Piccolo /
Flute

Oboe /
English Horn

Clarinet

Bassoon /
Bass Clarinet

French
Horns

Trumpets

Trombones /
Tuba

Timpani

Percussion

Violin I

Violin II

Violas

Cellos

Basses

Piccolo /
Flute

Oboe /
English Horn

Clarinet

Bassoon /
Bass Clarinet

French
Horns

Trumpets

Trombones /
Tuba

Timpani

Percussion

Violin I

Violin II

Violas

Cellos

Basses

Piccolo /
Flute

Oboe /
English Horn

Clarinet

Bassoon /
Bass Clarinet

French
Horns

Trumpets

Trombones /
Tuba

Timpani

Percussion

Violin I

Violin II

Violas

Cellos

Basses

Piccolo /
Flute

Oboe /
English Horn

Clarinet

Bassoon /
Bass Clarinet

French
Horns

Trumpets

Trombones /
Tuba

Timpani

Percussion

Violin I

Violin II

Violas

Cellos

Basses

Piccolo /
Flute

Oboe /
English Horn

Clarinet

Bassoon /
Bass Clarinet

French
Horns

Trumpets

Trombones /
Tuba

Timpani

Percussion

Violin I

Violin II

Violas

Cellos

Basses

Piccolo /
Flute

Oboe /
English Horn

Clarinet

Bassoon /
Bass Clarinet

French
Horns

Trumpets

Trombones /
Tuba

Timpani

Percussion

Violin I

Violin II

Violas

Cellos

Basses

Piccolo /
Flute

Oboe /
English Horn

Clarinet

Bassoon /
Bass Clarinet

French
Horns

Trumpets

Trombones /
Tuba

Timpani

Percussion

Violin I

Violin II

Violas

Cellos

Basses

Piccolo /
Flute

Oboe /
English Horn

Clarinet

Bassoon /
Bass Clarinet

French
Horns

Trumpets

Trombones /
Tuba

Timpani

Percussion

Violin I

Violin II

Violas

Cellos

Basses

Piccolo /
Flute

Oboe /
English Horn

Clarinet

Bassoon /
Bass Clarinet

French
Horns

Trumpets

Trombones /
Tuba

Timpani

Percussion

Violin I

Violin II

Violas

Cellos

Basses

Piccolo /
Flute

Oboe /
English Horn

Clarinet

Bassoon /
Bass Clarinet

French
Horns

Trumpets

Trombones /
Tuba

Timpani

Percussion

Violin I

Violin II

Violas

Cellos

Basses

Piccolo /
Flute

Oboe /
English Horn

Clarinet

Bassoon /
Bass Clarinet

French
Horns

Trumpets

Trombones /
Tuba

Timpani

Percussion

Violin I

Violin II

Violas

Cellos

Basses

Piccolo /
Flute

Oboe /
English Horn

Clarinet

Bassoon /
Bass Clarinet

French
Horns

Trumpets

Trombones /
Tuba

Timpani

Percussion

Violin I

Violin II

Violas

Cellos

Basses

Piccolo /
Flute

Oboe /
English Horn

Clarinet

Bassoon /
Bass Clarinet

French
Horns

Trumpets

Trombones /
Tuba

Timpani

Percussion

Violin I

Violin II

Violas

Cellos

Basses

Piccolo /
Flute

Oboe /
English Horn

Clarinet

Bassoon /
Bass Clarinet

French
Horns

Trumpets

Trombones /
Tuba

Timpani

Percussion

Violin I

Violin II

Violas

Cellos

Basses

Piccolo /
Flute

Oboe /
English Horn

Clarinet

Bassoon /
Bass Clarinet

French
Horns

Trumpets

Trombones /
Tuba

Timpani

Percussion

Violin I

Violin II

Violas

Cellos

Basses

Piccolo /
Flute

Oboe /
English Horn

Clarinet

Bassoon /
Bass Clarinet

French
Horns

Trumpets

Trombones /
Tuba

Timpani

Percussion

Violin I

Violin II

Violas

Cellos

Basses

Piccolo /
Flute

Oboe /
English Horn

Clarinet

Bassoon /
Bass Clarinet

French
Horns

Trumpets

Trombones /
Tuba

Timpani

Percussion

Violin I

Violin II

Violas

Cellos

Basses

Piccolo /
Flute

Oboe /
English Horn

Clarinet

Bassoon /
Bass Clarinet

French
Horns

Trumpets

Trombones /
Tuba

Timpani

Percussion

Violin I

Violin II

Violas

Cellos

Basses

Piccolo /
Flute

Oboe /
English Horn

Clarinet

Bassoon /
Bass Clarinet

French
Horns

Trumpets

Trombones /
Tuba

Timpani

Percussion

Violin I

Violin II

Violas

Cellos

Basses

Piccolo /
Flute

Oboe /
English Horn

Clarinet

Bassoon /
Bass Clarinet

French
Horns

Trumpets

Trombones /
Tuba

Timpani

Percussion

Violin I

Violin II

Violas

Cellos

Basses

Piccolo /
Flute

Oboe /
English Horn

Clarinet

Bassoon /
Bass Clarinet

French
Horns

Trumpets

Trombones /
Tuba

Timpani

Percussion

Violin I

Violin II

Violas

Cellos

Basses

Piccolo /
Flute

Oboe /
English Horn

Clarinet

Bassoon /
Bass Clarinet

French
Horns

Trumpets

Trombones /
Tuba

Timpani

Percussion

Violin I

Violin II

Violas

Cellos

Basses

Piccolo /
Flute

Oboe /
English Horn

Clarinet

Bassoon /
Bass Clarinet

French
Horns

Trumpets

Trombones /
Tuba

Timpani

Percussion

Violin I

Violin II

Violas

Cellos

Basses

Piccolo /
Flute

Oboe /
English Horn

Clarinet

Bassoon /
Bass Clarinet

French
Horns

Trumpets

Trombones /
Tuba

Timpani

Percussion

Violin I

Violin II

Violas

Cellos

Basses

Piccolo /
Flute

Oboe /
English Horn

Clarinet

Bassoon /
Bass Clarinet

French
Horns

Trumpets

Trombones /
Tuba

Timpani

Percussion

Violin I

Violin II

Violas

Cellos

Basses

Piccolo /
Flute

Oboe /
English Horn

Clarinet

Bassoon /
Bass Clarinet

French
Horns

Trumpets

Trombones /
Tuba

Timpani

Percussion

Violin I

Violin II

Violas

Cellos

Basses

Piccolo /
Flute

Oboe /
English Horn

Clarinet

Bassoon /
Bass Clarinet

French
Horns

Trumpets

Trombones /
Tuba

Timpani

Percussion

Violin I

Violin II

Violas

Cellos

Basses

Piccolo /
Flute

Oboe /
English Horn

Clarinet

Bassoon /
Bass Clarinet

French
Horns

Trumpets

Trombones /
Tuba

Timpani

Percussion

Violin I

Violin II

Violas

Cellos

Basses

Piccolo /
Flute

Oboe /
English Horn

Clarinet

Bassoon /
Bass Clarinet

French
Horns

Trumpets

Trombones /
Tuba

Timpani

Percussion

Violin I

Violin II

Violas

Cellos

Basses

Piccolo /
Flute

Oboe /
English Horn

Clarinet

Bassoon /
Bass Clarinet

French
Horns

Trumpets

Trombones /
Tuba

Timpani

Percussion

Violin I

Violin II

Violas

Cellos

Basses

Piccolo /
Flute

Oboe /
English Horn

Clarinet

Bassoon /
Bass Clarinet

French
Horns

Trumpets

Trombones /
Tuba

Timpani

Percussion

Violin I

Violin II

Violas

Cellos

Basses

Piccolo / Flute

Oboe / English Horn

Clarinet

Bassoon / Bass Clarinet

French Horns

Trumpets

Trombones / Tuba

Timpani

Percussion

Violin I

Violin II

Violas

Cellos

Basses

Piccolo /
Flute

Oboe /
English Horn

Clarinet

Bassoon /
Bass Clarinet

French
Horns

Trumpets

Trombones /
Tuba

Timpani

Percussion

Violin I

Violin II

Violas

Cellos

Basses

Piccolo /
Flute

Oboe /
English Horn

Clarinet

Bassoon /
Bass Clarinet

French
Horns

Trumpets

Trombones /
Tuba

Timpani

Percussion

Violin I

Violin II

Violas

Cellos

Basses

Piccolo /
Flute

Oboe /
English Horn

Clarinet

Bassoon /
Bass Clarinet

French
Horns

Trumpets

Trombones /
Tuba

Timpani

Percussion

Violin I

Violin II

Violas

Cellos

Basses

Piccolo /
Flute

Oboe /
English Horn

Clarinet

Bassoon /
Bass Clarinet

French
Horns

Trumpets

Trombones /
Tuba

Timpani

Percussion

Violin I

Violin II

Violas

Cellos

Basses

Piccolo /
Flute

Oboe /
English Horn

Clarinet

Bassoon /
Bass Clarinet

French
Horns

Trumpets

Trombones /
Tuba

Timpani

Percussion

Violin I

Violin II

Violas

Cellos

Basses

Piccolo /
Flute

Oboe /
English Horn

Clarinet

Bassoon /
Bass Clarinet

French
Horns

Trumpets

Trombones /
Tuba

Timpani

Percussion

Violin I

Violin II

Violas

Cellos

Basses

Piccolo /
Flute

Oboe /
English Horn

Clarinet

Bassoon /
Bass Clarinet

French
Horns

Trumpets

Trombones /
Tuba

Timpani

Percussion

Violin I

Violin II

Violas

Cellos

Basses

Piccolo /
Flute

Oboe /
English Horn

Clarinet

Bassoon /
Bass Clarinet

French
Horns

Trumpets

Trombones /
Tuba

Timpani

Percussion

Violin I

Violin II

Violas

Cellos

Basses

Piccolo /
Flute

Oboe /
English Horn

Clarinet

Bassoon /
Bass Clarinet

French
Horns

Trumpets

Trombones /
Tuba

Timpani

Percussion

Violin I

Violin II

Violas

Cellos

Basses

Piccolo /
Flute

Oboe /
English Horn

Clarinet

Bassoon /
Bass Clarinet

French
Horns

Trumpets

Trombones /
Tuba

Timpani

Percussion

Violin I

Violin II

Violas

Cellos

Basses

SCORE: ORCH-04

Piccolo /
Flute

Oboe /
English Horn

Clarinet

Bassoon /
Bass Clarinet

French
Horns

Trumpets

Trombones /
Tuba

Timpani

Percussion

Violin I

Violin II

Violas

Cellos

Basses

Piccolo /
Flute

Oboe /
English Horn

Clarinet

Bassoon /
Bass Clarinet

French
Horns

Trumpets

Trombones /
Tuba

Timpani

Percussion

Violin I

Violin II

Violas

Cellos

Basses

Piccolo /
Flute

Oboe /
English Horn

Clarinet

Bassoon /
Bass Clarinet

French
Horns

Trumpets

Trombones /
Tuba

Timpani

Percussion

Violin I

Violin II

Violas

Cellos

Basses

Piccolo /
Flute

Oboe /
English Horn

Clarinet

Bassoon /
Bass Clarinet

French
Horns

Trumpets

Trombones /
Tuba

Timpani

Percussion

Violin I

Violin II

Violas

Cellos

Basses

Piccolo /
Flute

Oboe /
English Horn

Clarinet

Bassoon /
Bass Clarinet

French
Horns

Trumpets

Trombones /
Tuba

Timpani

Percussion

Violin I

Violin II

Violas

Cellos

Basses

Piccolo /
Flute

Oboe /
English Horn

Clarinet

Bassoon /
Bass Clarinet

French
Horns

Trumpets

Trombones /
Tuba

Timpani

Percussion

Violin I

Violin II

Violas

Cellos

Basses

Piccolo / Flute

Oboe / English Horn

Clarinet

Bassoon / Bass Clarinet

French Horns

Trumpets

Trombones / Tuba

Timpani

Percussion

Violin I

Violin II

Violas

Cellos

Basses

Piccolo /
Flute

Oboe /
English Horn

Clarinet

Bassoon /
Bass Clarinet

French
Horns

Trumpets

Trombones /
Tuba

Timpani

Percussion

Violin I

Violin II

Violas

Cellos

Basses

Piccolo /
Flute

Oboe /
English Horn

Clarinet

Bassoon /
Bass Clarinet

French
Horns

Trumpets

Trombones /
Tuba

Timpani

Percussion

Violin I

Violin II

Violas

Cellos

Basses

Piccolo /
Flute

Oboe /
English Horn

Clarinet

Bassoon /
Bass Clarinet

French
Horns

Trumpets

Trombones /
Tuba

Timpani

Percussion

Violin I

Violin II

Violas

Cellos

Basses

Piccolo /
Flute

Oboe /
English Horn

Clarinet

Bassoon /
Bass Clarinet

French
Horns

Trumpets

Trombones /
Tuba

Timpani

Percussion

Violin I

Violin II

Violas

Cellos

Basses

Piccolo /
Flute

Oboe /
English Horn

Clarinet

Bassoon /
Bass Clarinet

French
Horns

Trumpets

Trombones /
Tuba

Timpani

Percussion

Violin I

Violin II

Violas

Cellos

Basses

Piccolo /
Flute

Oboe /
English Horn

Clarinet

Bassoon /
Bass Clarinet

French
Horns

Trumpets

Trombones /
Tuba

Timpani

Percussion

Violin I

Violin II

Violas

Cellos

Basses

Piccolo /
Flute

Oboe /
English Horn

Clarinet

Bassoon /
Bass Clarinet

French
Horns

Trumpets

Trombones /
Tuba

Timpani

Percussion

Violin I

Violin II

Violas

Cellos

Basses

Piccolo / Flute
Oboe / English Horn
Clarinet
Bassoon / Bass Clarinet
French Horns
Trumpets
Trombones / Tuba
Timpani
Percussion
Violin I
Violin II
Violas
Cellos
Basses

Piccolo /
Flute

Oboe /
English Horn

Clarinet

Bassoon /
Bass Clarinet

French
Horns

Trumpets

Trombones /
Tuba

Timpani

Percussion

Violin I

Violin II

Violas

Cellos

Basses

Piccolo /
Flute

Oboe /
English Horn

Clarinet

Bassoon /
Bass Clarinet

French
Horns

Trumpets

Trombones /
Tuba

Timpani

Percussion

Violin I

Violin II

Violas

Cellos

Basses

Piccolo / Flute

Oboe / English Horn

Clarinet

Bassoon / Bass Clarinet

French Horns

Trumpets

Trombones / Tuba

Timpani

Percussion

Violin I

Violin II

Violas

Cellos

Basses

Piccolo /
Flute

Oboe /
English Horn

Clarinet

Bassoon /
Bass Clarinet

French
Horns

Trumpets

Trombones /
Tuba

Timpani

Percussion

Violin I

Violin II

Violas

Cellos

Basses

Piccolo /
Flute

Oboe /
English Horn

Clarinet

Bassoon /
Bass Clarinet

French
Horns

Trumpets

Trombones /
Tuba

Timpani

Percussion

Violin I

Violin II

Violas

Cellos

Basses

Piccolo /
Flute

Oboe /
English Horn

Clarinet

Bassoon /
Bass Clarinet

French
Horns

Trumpets

Trombones /
Tuba

Timpani

Percussion

Violin I

Violin II

Violas

Cellos

Basses

Piccolo /
Flute

Oboe /
English Horn

Clarinet

Bassoon /
Bass Clarinet

French
Horns

Trumpets

Trombones /
Tuba

Timpani

Percussion

Violin I

Violin II

Violas

Cellos

Basses

Piccolo /
Flute

Oboe /
English Horn

Clarinet

Bassoon /
Bass Clarinet

French
Horns

Trumpets

Trombones /
Tuba

Timpani

Percussion

Violin I

Violin II

Violas

Cellos

Basses

Piccolo /
Flute

Oboe /
English Horn

Clarinet

Bassoon /
Bass Clarinet

French
Horns

Trumpets

Trombones /
Tuba

Timpani

Percussion

Violin I

Violin II

Violas

Cellos

Basses

Piccolo /
Flute

Oboe /
English Horn

Clarinet

Bassoon /
Bass Clarinet

French
Horns

Trumpets

Trombones /
Tuba

Timpani

Percussion

Violin I

Violin II

Violas

Cellos

Basses

Piccolo /
Flute

Oboe /
English Horn

Clarinet

Bassoon /
Bass Clarinet

French
Horns

Trumpets

Trombones /
Tuba

Timpani

Percussion

Violin I

Violin II

Violas

Cellos

Basses